DAVID COLBERT

10
DAYS

MARTIN LUTHER
KING JR.

ALADDIN P

NEW YORK LONDON

ALADDIN PAPERBACKS • An imprint of Simon & Schuster Children's Publishing Division • 1230 Avenue of the Americas, New York, NY 10020 • Text copyright © 2008 by David Colbert • The photographs in this book are under copyright and are reprinted here with permission of the owners. All rights reserved. • All rights reserved, including the right of reproduction in whole or in part in any form. • ALADDIN PAPERBACKS and related logo are registered trademarks of Simon & Schuster, Inc. • Cover and interior designed by Karin Paprocki • Special thanks to David Lancaster, whose name should be on this book, for his exemplary work, and to John Chew for his mathematical expertise. • The text of this book was set in Perpetua. • Manufactured in the United States of America • First Aladdin Paperbacks edition November 2008 • 10 9 8 7 6 5 4 3 2 1 • Library of Congress Control Number 2008936765 • ISBN-13: 978-1-4169-6805-4 • ISBN-10: 1-4169-6805-9

CONTENTS

INTRODUCTION

One person more than any other showed the millions of Americans who sacrificed for the civil rights movement a reason to hope and a way forward.

DAY 1:
APRIL 17, 1944
CONTEST

Growing up in the South, King comes face to face with the injustice of segregation.

DAY 2:
DECEMBER 5, 1955
BOYCOTT

After Rosa Parks is arrested for refusing to give up her seat on a city bus, King leads a bus boycott.

DAY 3:
MAY 28, 1960
THE VERDICT

King defends himself against charges of tax fraud as he inspires students to begin a new kind of protest.

INTRODUCTION

The civil rights movement succeeded because it had many brave organizers and supporters. Hundreds of men and women started local protests and initiatives that grew to national importance. Thousands—perhaps millions—risked their lives.

And yet there's a lot of truth in the notion that Martin Luther King Jr. was special, a first among equals. He set an extraordinary challenge for himself and his movement: to achieve through peaceful victories what would have been difficult even for someone who used threats or violence. He was determined to change the minds of his opponents, not merely defeat them. King's adherence to the ideal of nonviolence was all the more admirable because he and his supporters faced so much violence themselves, often from the very law enforcement officers who should have been offering protection. It would have been easy to strike back. King refused to do that, and urged his colleagues to be equally as disciplined.

Despite being the focus of so much adoration, no one was more aware of the work done by others than King himself. One man who knew him said King "felt keenly that people who had done as much as he had or *more* got no such tribute. This troubled him deeply because there's no way of sharing that kind of tribute with anyone else: You can't give it away; you have to accept it. But when you don't feel you're worthy of it and you're an honest, principled man, it tortures you.

And it could be said that he was tortured by the great appreciation the public showed for him."

King judged himself harshly and, despite his great achievements, was consumed by the work left to do. His murder, not long after his thirty-ninth birthday, left more work than he imagined. But the extraordinary changes in the United States that continue to take place since his death—the changes that he dreamed of—are proof of his lasting influence. In his relatively short life, just 14,325 days, these ten days changed his world and yours.

CONTEST

Franklinton, Georgia.

"Y ou need to get up, now," the bus driver says, looking at fifteen-year-old Martin Luther King Jr. "These other folks need to sit down."

M. L. (that's what everybody calls him) stares straight ahead. *Why?* M. L. thinks. *Why should I have to get up?* But of course he knows the reason. He's black, and white people want his seat. They *expect* it.

He knows what can happen to African Americans

who refuse to obey the bus laws. He knows they can be forced off the bus or even arrested. He has seen blacks savagely beaten for less. He looks out the window and sees the sign at the bus stop: FRANKLINTON. He's ninety miles away from Atlanta and home.

"You need to get up," the bus driver repeats angrily. He sees only a black teenager—a *disobedient* black teenager. In the culture of the South, that's all that matters. It doesn't matter than this young man plays the violin, enjoys opera, excels at sports, and earns top grades in high school, where he has already skipped one grade and will later skip his senior year. It doesn't matter that M. L. is a minister's son who lives in a household with rules, expectations, and discipline; or that he goes to church all day on Sunday and almost every other day of the week; or that he's often dressed as he is today, in a smart suit. It doesn't even matter that earlier today M. L. represented his school at a statewide oratory contest.

There's no innocent explanation for the driver's

demand: He's not merely asking a polite young man to give up his seat for an older person. One of M. L.'s teachers, Sarah Grace Bradley, who has accompanied M. L. to the contest, is also being told to move.

JIM CROW

Usually M. L. is treated like a prince. He's a member of the affluent and educated elite of Atlanta, one of the most important cities in African American life. Nearly half of Atlanta's 300,000 citizens are African American. The city is home to some of the nation's best black colleges—Clark, Morehouse, Spelman, and Atlanta University—which have attracted intellectuals like the prominent scholar W. E. B. Du Bois. Economically, the black community ranges from business tycoons to sharecroppers. Socially, there's no more important institution in black Atlanta than the church, and the church where M. L.'s father is pastor, Ebenezer Baptist, has been at the center of the community for three generations. M. L. and his older sister and younger brother are well known within the community because of their father's position. They're aware that their family has many advantages not shared by the many black citizens of Atlanta who are kept from well-paying jobs because of racism. But neither their social status nor their affluence protects them from bigotry. M. L. has known it all his life. When he was five, the father of his best friend, a white boy, had forbidden his son to play with M. L. because M. L. was black. M. L. never forgot the shock of that first lesson in racism.

M. L. has inherited his father's ability to captivate an audience, and it was no surprise that a few days earlier he won a spot at the oratory contest. By this time, the subject of his speech was also no surprise: He was already furious at the injustices Southern blacks faced, and the poverty that resulted from it. The title of his speech was "The Negro and the Constitution." It called for the full enforcement of laws already in the U.S. Constitution that should have guaranteed equality for African Americans. It demanded access to education, jobs, and health care, all of which were kept from African Americans by local laws—which the Constitution should have overruled—that maintained segregation.

Those laws were known casually as "Jim Crow." The name came from a character in minstrel shows, a popular entertainment that made fun of African Americans, portraying them as lazy, stupid, and superstitious. White actors played Jim Crow in "blackface" (dark, clownish makeup). There were Jim Crow laws against eating in the same restaurants, drinking from the same water fountains, swimming in the same pools, and, of course, sitting together on buses.

> THOMAS D. RICE (1808–1860) CREATED THE 1828 SONG AND DANCE ROUTINE "JUMP JIM CROW." HE WAS MIMICKING AN AFRICAN AMERICAN STREET PERFORMER.

The first Jim Crow laws were passed a few decades after the Civil War, when political compromises allowed Southern states to reestablish some of the local power they had lost when they lost the war. The laws ignored the Thirteenth, Fourteenth, and Fifteenth Amendments to the U.S. Constitution, passed after the war, guaranteeing that blacks were free, that they would receive equal protection under the law, and that they could vote.

Jim Crow laws were designed specifically to make sure blacks stayed poor, uneducated, and utterly powerless to change their circumstances. They also kept the two races physically separated in public. Hypocritically, it was common for even the most admired men in the white community to have relationships with African American women, and these were usually ignored by friends provided the man was discreet. For example, Strom Thurmond, a governor of South Carolina and then a senator from the state, who actually ran for president of the United States in

A segregated movie theater in Florida. This is the back entrance. The front entrance was reserved for white patrons. Inside theaters like this one, African Americans were segregated into the balcony.

1948 on a segregationist platform, had a secret daughter who resulted from his relationship with a family maid. This was only made public after his death in the year 2003—when his daughter was almost seventy-eight years old. (Thurmond lived to just less than 101 years.)

In his speech, M. L. warned that that the whole nation suffers from segregation: "We cannot have an enlightened democracy with one great group living in ignorance. We cannot have a healthy nation with one tenth of the people ill-nourished, sick, harboring germs of disease which recognize no color lines, obey no Jim Crow laws."

M. L. delivered the speech in his ringing baritone entirely from memory, without looking at any notes. It was a heartfelt speech that had passionately named the abuses suffered by Southern blacks and the remedy for those abuses: fair play and free opportunity. And it had won. Now he feels that this bus driver wants to take that success away from him.

DADDY KING

The bus driver is demanding: "Give these white folks your seat."

What would Daddy do? M. L. wonders. His father, Martin Luther King Sr., the single most influential person in M. L.'s life, does everything he can to resist the unjust social order. M. L. remembers the day "Daddy King" was pulled over by a policeman for a traffic violation. "Boy," the patrolman had demanded, "show me your license." As a holdover from days of slavery, white people in the South commonly called African American men of any age by the condescending term "boy."

"Do you see this child here?" Daddy had retorted, pointing to M. L. "That's a boy there. I'm a *man*. I'm *Reverend* King."

Reverend King had arrived at his station in life by his own intelligence, ambition, and hard work. Growing up as a sharecropper's son, he had seen the very worst that the Jim Crow South inflicted on former slaves and their descendants. He saw whites humiliate blacks, beat them, and even lynch them—hang them by the neck from trees until they were dead—without being punished.

> A SHARE-CROPPER IS A FARMER WHO RENTS LAND BY GIVING THE OWNER A PORTION, USUALLY HALF, OF WHAT'S GROWN. IT'S A COMMON PRACTICE WHERE MONEY IS SCARCE.

Reverend King also overcame family difficulties. He had watched his father regularly beat his mother after drinking too much. When he was fifteen, he defended her by wrestling his father to the floor. The next day his father pledged never to beat his mother again.

Not long afterward, Mike (he later changed his name to Martin Luther) left for Atlanta, determined to rise in the world. He went to school at night, earning his high school diploma and later a degree in divinity. He refused to ride the segregated buses in Atlanta, and bought a car as soon as he could afford one.

He courted and married Alberta Williams, the daughter of Reverend Adam Daniel Williams, pastor of Ebenezer Baptist Church. When Reverend Williams died in 1931, Reverend King took over as pastor of Ebenezer. He was widely known for his fiery sermons, which M. L. sometimes found embarrassing.

By this time Reverend King had built a reputation for himself as a man of integrity, wisdom, and influence. Even white leaders in Atlanta sought his counsel in matters of race. He never hesitated to assert his rights as he understood them. "I don't care how long I have to live with the system," he said, "I am never going to accept it. I'll fight it until I die."

M. L. sits in his seat, staring straight ahead, not moving a muscle. He knows exactly what his father would be thinking in the same situation. *There's no reason for me to give up my seat.*

The bus driver loses his patience and begins to swear at M. L., but M. L. doesn't move. *I don't want to fight this man*, M. L. thinks, *but I will if I have to.*

Then he feels his teacher take his hand and turns to see her imploring eyes filled with fear. "We have to obey the law," she whispers. M. L. can't do that—he can't respect this law. But he can respect his teacher. In deference to her, he slowly stands up.

Some of M. L.'s remarks in his speech earlier this day perfectly describe what's happening now, just a few hours after the ringing applause in the auditorium: "The finest Negro is at the mercy of the meanest white man. Even winners of our highest honors face the class color bar. . . . [W]ith their right hand [white Americans] raise to high places the great who have dark skins, and with their left, they slap us down to keep us in 'our places.' "

The bus fills completely. With no seats available, M. L. and his teacher stand for the last ninety miles of the trip home to Atlanta. Years later he would tell people this moment was the angriest he had ever been in his life. ❶

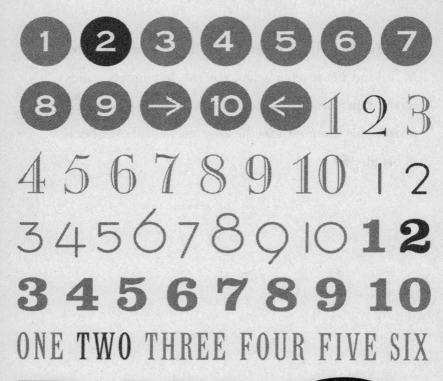

ONE **TWO** THREE FOUR FIVE SIX

DAY 2

TWO

DECEMBER 5,

1955

BOYCOTT

Montgomery, Alabama.

Twenty-six-year-old Martin Luther King Jr. jumps into his car and rushes to the Holt Street Baptist Church on this chilly evening. He knows a crowd is waiting—a crowd that has suddenly asked him to lead them into a dangerous situation. He's prepared for what he sees as he gets close to the church: A traffic jam blocks the last five blocks of the trip because so many people have come to hear what he has to tell to them. Parking his car, he walks the rest of the way to the church and politely moves through the crowd waiting outside, which reaches the sidewalk. They're congratulating him even before he begins to speak. They have no idea that even just twenty minutes ago the awesome responsibility had left him at a loss for words. But this whole day has been extraordinary, and he's determined to live up to expectations. Starting early this morning, the African Americans in this city—half of the population—chose to say, *No more Jim Crow. We've had enough.* They began an extraordinary protest. Then, just a few hours ago, King, relatively new to Montgomery, where he'd come to be pastor of the Dexter Avenue Baptist Church, was put in charge of leading this courageous movement. In an instant, the course of his life has changed. The pastor of a small Southern church will soon be a national figure.

Luckily, King has thought for a long time about the ideas he is about to express, and for years he has unconsciously prepared for moment just like this one.

THE GOOD SHEPHERD

King has come a long way since that angry bus ride back from the oratory contest. In the summer after that incident, he worked on a tobacco farm in Connecticut, and for the first time in his life experienced the blissful absence of segregation. He sat in the same theaters as white people and ate in the same restaurants. On the train ride home, however, when the train reached Washington, D.C., he had to switch to a black car to continue the ride through the segregated South. He found it all the more disturbing because the change occurred in the nation's capital.

When he was only fifteen, he enrolled in Morehouse College, thinking he might like to become a doctor or a lawyer. In his last year at Morehouse, however, he decided to become a minister. It seemed to be the best way he could help his people, and it would take advantage of his remarkable oratorical gifts. To further his education he enrolled at Crozer Theological Seminary in Pennsylvania. There he learned about philosophers who had struggled with the same kind of injustice that angered him. He espe-cially liked the ideas of Henry David Thoreau, who argued that moral people should disobey immoral laws by performing acts of "civil disobedience." Thoreau seemed to be saying that it was not just the right but the *duty* to dis-obey laws like the Jim Crow stat-utes of the Southern states. King was impressed that Thoreau had been willing to go to jail for his beliefs. Then in the spring of 1950, King heard a lecture about Mahatma Gandhi, who had led the people of India to freedom from British rule without firing a single shot. Gandhi had encour-aged his people to protest without violence, as a way

> "UNDER A GOVERNMENT WHICH IMPRISONS ANY UNJUSTLY, THE TRUE PLACE FOR A JUST MAN IS ALSO A PRISON."
> —HENRY DAVID THOREAU, "CIVIL DISOBEDIENCE"

to shame the British into acknowledging the immorality of their oppression. After many protests and seven years in prison, Gandhi proved successful. King read as much as he could about Gandhi in the hope that he had found a way to defeat the Jim Crow laws he despised.

King graduated from Crozer at the head of his class, and decided to go to Boston University to earn a doctorate in theology. There, at the suggestion of a friend, he introduced himself to Coretta Scott, a music student from Alabama. Within one hour of meeting her, King declared she had everything he looked for in a wife: character, intelligence, personality, and beauty. One year later, they were married.

Soon afterward, the Kings faced a difficult decision. Malcolm was offered jobs in northern states, and Coretta was certain her music career would go further there. They were both happy to get away from the insulting segregation of the South, and, thinking ahead to a family, they wanted their future children to be spared that system. But something in both of them wanted to fight segregation rather than escape it. They believed they had an obligation to serve those people who couldn't escape segregation as easily as they could.

They ended up not just in the South but in the first capital of the Confederacy. The Dexter Avenue Baptist Church stands across a public square from the Alabama State capitol, where, King knew before he first visited his potential home, Jefferson Davis had been sworn in as president of the Confederate States of America. "Here the first Confederate flag was made and unfurled," King later wrote. "I was to see this imposing reminder of the Confederacy from the steps of the Dexter Avenue Baptist Church many times in the following years."

I n May 1954, just as King was taking his post at Dexter, the Supreme Court announced a decision that offered hope to those fighting Jim Crow. In the case of *Brown v. Board of Education of Topeka*, the court ruled that racial segregation of schools was illegal.

That decision was the reverse of one the court had made more than fifty years earlier, in a case called *Plessy v. Ferguson*, which had allowed separate facilities for blacks and whites. The *Plessy* decision said the separate facilities merely had to be equal. In the *Brown* decision, the justices said that separate public schools based on race were, for all practical purposes, unequal, and therefore unconstitutional. It ordered the schools to integrate.

> **THURGOOD MARSHALL, ONE OF THE LAWYERS WHO WON THE *Brown* CASE, WAS APPOINTED A FEDERAL JUDGE IN 1961 AND WAS RAISED TO THE SUPREME COURT IN 1967.**

Black leaders knew that the *Brown* decision made all of the segregation laws vulnerable to revocation. They began to make plans for new legal challenges against racism.

In Montgomery, one of the most prominent leaders was E. D. Nixon, who, despite just a year of formal schooling, had long been leading effective local protests. Among his many positions, he was president of the Montgomery chapter of the National Association for the Advancement of Colored People (NAACP), one of the most effective civil rights organizations. (The NAACP had been the driving force in the several court cases that led to the *Brown* decision.) Nixon and other black leaders decided to mount a campaign against the bus laws, which in Montgomery were even worse than what King had experienced on the ride through Georgia. For example, African Americans in Montgomery had to enter at the front door of a bus to pay the driver, then step back out of the bus, walk to the back door, and reenter there.

Maybe the most absurd fact about this treatment is that three-fourths of the riders on Montgomery buses were black. They should have been treated as the best customers. But that was also a weakness in Jim Crow. Nixon and his colleagues knew that if blacks refused to ride the buses, the bus company would lose a lot of money. If the boycott lasted long enough, the bus company might be forced to accept the protesters' demands for better treatment.

Nixon also wanted a strong court case against the bus company. For that, he needed to identify an individual case of mistreatment that proved the illegal inequity of the bus company policies toward African Americans. That case came to him by way of an old friend and colleague, an officer of the Montgomery NAACP, Rosa Parks.

Parks, like many Southern blacks, had conducted a lifelong battle against Jim Crow. She understood the bus laws all too well. Once, after paying her fare at the front of the bus, she had refused the driver's order to get off and reenter at the back door, and she had been physically thrown off.

On December 1, 1955, Parks, a seamstress, finished work and boarded the bus in downtown Montgomery. Following the Jim Crow rules, she sat just behind the section reserved for whites. But then the bus filled up, and when a white man could not find a seat, the driver asked Parks to give up hers.

Parks refused, silently.

"Look, woman," the bus driver said, "I told you I wanted the seat. Are you going to stand up?"

Parks knew that if blacks were ever going to begin the long journey to equality, someone had to take the first step. She knew she could be ejected, jailed, or even beaten. But she'd had enough. She looked at the bus driver and uttered a single word: "No."

She was taken off the bus and arrested. By the time she arrived at the police station, news of her arrest had already reached Nixon, who immediately decided, *This is the case.*

O ver the weekend Nixon and other black leaders, including King, hastily organized the boycott of the bus system. They sent out thousands of leaflets encouraging blacks not to ride the buses on Monday. They specified three demands: for bus drivers to be polite, for blacks not to have to get up for whites, and for blacks to be able to apply for jobs as bus drivers.

King wondered if this rushed protest would work. He knew that for some people, boycotting the bus could mean missing work and possibly losing a job. Monday morning, he drove all around the city, from bus stop to bus stop, to see how many people would feel they had to ignore the boycott. To his astonishment, bus stops all over the city were empty.

That afternoon black leaders met to discuss plans for continuing the boycott beyond the one day they'd planned. A new organization, the Montgomery

*Rosa Parks, in a police mug shot from a protest
during the Montgomery bus boycott*

Improvement Association (MIA), was established to
coordinate the boycott. King, new to the city and
therefore free of old political entanglements, was

unexpectedly chosen to be its head. The leaders then made a plan for a mass meeting a few hours later. King would speak, and if there was enough support from the community, the boycott would continue. The twenty-six-year-old had just been thrust into the most visible position in a protest that would involve the entire nation.

A LOVE SUPREME

Now, King steps up to the podium and stares out at more than a thousand faces, knowing that outside the church four thousand more people are listening over loudspeakers.

He now knows he doesn't need to urge the crowd to act. He doesn't have to wait until the speech is over to know the boycott will continue. What he needs to do, what he begins to do as he takes the microphone, is urge the people in the crowd to protest in a particular way——the nonviolent way.

As he finishes, the crowd rises as one to applaud him and his ideals.

Victory in the Montgomery bus boycott won't come as quickly as this day's events suggest, but it will come, after more than a year of difficulty and sacrifice by the African Americans of the city. Looking back from today's perspective, it may be surprising that the boycott had to last that long, but many white citizens of Montgomery were determined to fight integration to the end. King himself will become a target for their anger. Most days he'll receive death threats. A bomb will be exploded on his porch. Finally, the Supreme Court will issue a decision declaring Alabama's bus segregation laws unconstitutional.

On December 20, 1956——381 days after Rosa Parks was arrested——the boycott will end. At dawn the next day King and some of his colleagues in the boycott, trailed by reporters and television cameras, will board the city's first integrated bus.

As King steps on, the bus driver will say, "I believe you are Reverend King, aren't you?"

King will reply, "Yes, I am."

"We are glad," the driver will say politely, "to have you with us." ❷

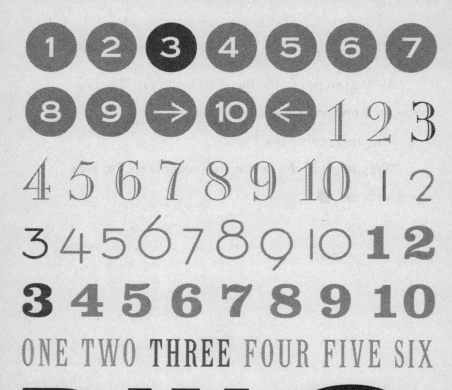

ONE TWO **THREE** FOUR FIVE SIX

DAY 3

MAY 28,

1960

THREE

THE VERDICT

County Courthouse, Montgomery, Alabama.

T hree months earlier: On a quiet weekday two sheriff's deputies enter Daddy King's Ebenezer Baptist Church in Atlanta, where young Martin, now thirty-one years old, has recently joined his father and taken the role of assistant pastor. The deputies have a warrant for Martin's arrest.

In Martin's office they tell him they're arresting him on behalf of the authorities in his old home state of Alabama. The charge is tax evasion.

King is furious. This arrest has nothing to do with taxes. This is about putting an end to his civil rights work. The Alabama government had already checked his old returns and had sent him a bill for extra taxes, which he had immediately paid. That's common. But now, because the information in his tax papers was wrong, the state is charging him under a serious part of the criminal code with lying in a sworn document. There's nothing common about that. He's the first person to be charged with felony tax evasion in the history of Alabama.

Is this how they're going to stop me? he wonders. Along with the anger he feels shame. He shouldn't have made this tax error in the first place. He's given the authorities a chance to question his character. He immediately understands they intend to make a spectacle of this case.

Now on this day in May, King is back in Alabama for the trial that's meant to destroy his public image and put him in jail. In the county courthouse, just a few blocks from his former congregation, the Dexter Avenue Baptist Church, he looks at the judge, a white man. He glances over at the prosecuting attorney on the other side of the courtroom—also white. He scans the faces of the twelve jurors who will determine his fate. All white. A sudden shudder of terror runs through his body. *How can I possibly get a fair trial? I was charged with this crime because I'm black. What chance do I have against twelve white men?*

He takes a deep breath and prepares himself for the inevitable worst.

"GIVE US THE BALLOT"

King is the authorities' target because of what has happened since the Montgomery bus boycott. In a movement with many leaders, he's the unofficial first among equals.

Following the success of the boycott, black leaders

formed the Southern Christian Leadership Conference (SCLC) to press for further gains. They elected King as its president.

The SCLC is focused on voting rights for blacks, who are kept from polls in the South with a variety of illegal methods like unusual tests and faraway registration offices with limited hours. King has traveled throughout the country and also abroad to expose these tactics of the Southern white establishment and to gain support for the civil rights movement.

Southern whites are feeling threatened by the criticism they're facing. State and local governments are determined to resist federal laws and the decisions of the Supreme Court. The desegregation order of the *Brown v. Board of Education of Topeka* ruling was very publicly ignored in a few states. President Eisenhower had to send the U.S. Army to protect black students as they went to classes at Central High School in Little Rock, Arkansas. (A few years from this date, in another famous incident, the governor of Alabama,

George Wallace, whose inauguration speech included the promise, "segregation now, segregation tomorrow, segregation forever," will stand in front of the door to a building at the University of Alabama to prevent two black students from enrolling. He'll have to be removed from the spot by federal marshals.)

Wherever he goes, King's message is simple: He wants the protection of the right to vote. If they could vote, he argues, blacks could abolish all the other unjust laws that oppressed them. "Give us the ballot," he said, "and we will quietly and nonviolently, without rancor or bitterness, implement the Supreme Court's decision [against segregation]."

With celebrity comes danger. At a bookstore in Harlem, where he's signing copies of his book about the Montgomery boycott, *Stride Toward Freedom*, a deranged fan stabs him in the chest with a letter opener and nearly kills him. The knife was so close to piercing his heart, his doctor later told him, that he would have died if he had merely sneezed, or if someone had tried to save him by removing the knife before the doctors could do it.

Another less obvious danger also comes with being the face of the movement: The book, speeches, and many traveling expenses create an accounting nightmare. Although King gives a lot of money to the organizations he supports, merely keeping track of what comes in and what goes out is far more difficult than when he received only his minister's salary at Dexter.

SIT-INS

One kind of accounting remains simple: The numbers of people taking part in civil protests increases every day. Now that King is in his thirties, he watches from a slight distance as a new generation of passionate and committed young people joins the struggle.

On February 1, 1960, four students at North

Carolina Agricultural and Technical College in Greensboro revived a simple form of protest that had been tried many years earlier in Chicago: They walked into a Woolworth store and sat down at the lunch counter.

They knew they would not be served. Even though blacks could shop in the rest of the store, the lunch counter was reserved for whites. They remained seated, however, and did their homework. If the store wanted to call the police, they could go right ahead. The manager didn't take the bait, but the protesters didn't budge. They stayed until the counter closed for the day.

The following day they came back with fifteen more black students. The next day, three hundred! Later in the protests as many as a thousand students showed up, each one ready to take the place of anyone who was arrested. The jail in Greensboro simply couldn't hold everyone willing to be arrested at the sit-in. It was exactly the kind of nonviolent protest

February 2, 1960: the second day of the sit-in protest at the Woolworth lunch counter in Greensboro, North Carolina. The section of the counter where the students are sitting is now preserved in the Smithsonian Institution. From left: Joseph McNeil, Franklin McCain, William Smith, and Clarence Henderson.

that King advocated, but the idea came from the students themselves.

King was invited to Durham, North Carolina to address students at a rally in support of the sit-ins. He was proud to accept. The commitment of the students inspired him. He believed the sit-ins represented the most important development in the civil rights movement up to that time. He told the students that democracy and segregation cannot exist together, and that they were fulfilling their duty to oppose inequality so that democracy might flourish. "Fill up the jails," he called out, as the students cheered.

He had no idea that while he was speaking in Durham, the authorities in Alabama had a jail cell in mind for him, too.

FEAR ON TRIAL

King was arrested right after he returned from visiting the sit-in protesters.

His lawyers gave him little reason to hope. They weren't entirely convinced he was innocent, and they were sure that the verdict was already planned by the jury and judge. That's just how it worked for black defendants in the South. The only question was, how much time would he serve in jail? He was facing ten years.

Then one of his lawyers, Chauncey Eskridge, took on the detailed arithmetic of clarifying King's finances, which would have to be discussed during the trial. He laboriously added and subtracted every entry in the diaries and figured out exactly how much money King had made, how much he had given away, and how much he actually owed in taxes. Maybe if the state had made an error and the amount was smaller than what King had already paid, the sentence would be less than the maximum.

The hardest part was understanding the taxes on what King gave away. The authorities were claiming that King had kept some of the money he said he'd donated.

"Fellas," Eskridge said to the other lawyers when he was finished, "I've got news for you. Dr. King didn't take any of that money." They looked at his figures. He was right. The evidence was on their side. Unfortunately, in some courtrooms the evidence doesn't matter.

The trial took three days, during which the prosecution introduced 999 pieces of evidence, mostly financial records. But King's lawyers managed to get a key prosecution witness to admit that he wasn't sure exactly how much money King had made. The witness also admitted he had once told King that there was no evidence of fraud in his tax return. But King knew the jury would convict him anyway.

TWELVE ANGRY MEN

During his lawyer's closing statements, King can't concentrate on what he's hearing. *Ten years*, he thinks. *Not for a crime of conscience. Not for a protest. For fraud.* They've already won.

The jury leaves the courtroom to decide the verdict. The *all-white* jury. Three hours and forty-five minutes later, they file back in. The foreman hands a piece of paper to the judge.

"The defendant will rise," the judge says. He looks at the piece of paper and back at King.

"Not guilty."

King can barely believe it. It can't be.

Outside the courthouse, he composes himself and addresses the reporters. "This represents great hope, and it shows that there are hundreds of thousands of white people of good will in the South, even though they may disagree with our views on integration."

King will later describe this struggle as a "turning point" in his life. The white power structure has done its best to bring him down, and it has failed.

It also can't stop the movement. The Greensboro sit-ins have already inspired sit-ins all over the country. White students are joining black students in the protest. A new organization of young protesters, the Student Nonviolent Coordinating Committee (SNCC), has been created. Its leaders and members will be an important part of what's soon to come. They'll continue to fire up King and drive him forward, just as they are inspired by him. As one of their leaders, John Lewis, tells the crowd at a sit-in, reminding them to endure the violence of the authorities without reacting in kind: "Remember the teachings of Jesus, Gandhi, Thoreau, and Martin Luther King Jr." ❸

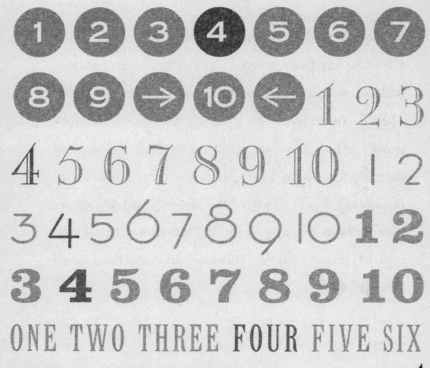

ONE TWO THREE **FOUR** FIVE SIX

DAY
FOUR
4

MAY 21,
1961

FREEDOM RIDERS

Montgomery, Alabama.

King steps off the airplane at the Montgomery airport and is immediately intercepted by fifty U.S. marshals. They aren't there to arrest him, but to protect him. Horrific violence has been inflicted on civil rights protesters in the past weeks, and the marshals have been sent there by U.S. Attorney General Robert Kennedy to make sure that King won't be harmed.

The marshals escort King to the home of Ralph

Abernathy, his closest friend and colleague since the days of the Montgomery bus boycott, who has been by King's side through nearly every protest. But King still isn't safe. He's about to endure one of the most harrowing nights of his life.

Seventeen days ago, on May 4, 1961, thirteen travelers boarded two buses to embark on what they called a Freedom Ride through the South, from Washington, D.C., to New Orleans. The Freedom

*The Reverend Ralph Abernathy, pictured here
at a 1968 National Press Club luncheon*

Riders, seven blacks and six whites, have come up with a courageous and intelligent protest against the lingering Jim Crow laws.

Because the federal government controls travel between states, it has the legal right to set rules for the buses on those routes. State law doesn't apply, so the white governments of Southern states can't protect the segregation that continues to exist on some interstate bus lines and even within bus stations. About half a year earlier, a Supreme Court decision, *Boynton v. Virginia*, had overturned the arrest of a black man who refused to a leave a "whites only" restaurant in a bus terminal.

The hard part is getting the federal government to enforce its authority over the states. That's what the Freedom Riders hope to do.

James Farmer, director of the Congress of Racial Equality (CORE), which organized the ride, later said, "We planned the Freedom Ride with the specific intention of creating a crisis. We figured that the government would have to respond if we created a situation that was headline news all over the world."

The Freedom Riders expected to be attacked. In that regard, they weren't disappointed.

GET ON THE BUS

The Riders were first attacked by a white mob in Rock Hill, South Carolina. SNCC leader John Lewis, who was one of the Riders, offered no resistance as he was beaten. Albert Bigelow, a white pacifist, did the same. The police only stepped in when a white female Rider was attacked.

Acting on reports that angry Ku Klux Klan members were lying in wait along the highway in Alabama, Attorney General Robert Kennedy, the brother of President John F. Kennedy, tried to get Alabama Governor John Patterson to protect the Riders as they traveled through his state. Patterson, a segregationist,

wanted to refuse, but to keep the federal government away, he agreed to offer local protection. At the
same time, he secretly
made arrangements for
a judge's order to stop
the rides.

Governor Patterson
had helped to elect
President Kennedy, so
the Kennedys didn't
want a confrontation
with him. They had the
same concerns about
other Southern politi-

Marion S. Trikosko / Library of Congress

cians. Although they agreed

John Lewis at a 1964 meeting

with the goals of the civil

of the American Society of

rights movement, their

Newspaper Editors

Democratic Party received some of its strongest support in the South, and the Kennedys didn't want to
lose that support. They hoped the protesters would be

more patient and let them try more subtle approaches. They resented being forced to choose between enforcing the federal laws, which cost them support in the South, and ignoring the violence, which made them look weak. Of course, forcing that choice was the point of the protests.

ALL THE PRESIDENT'S MEN

When the Riders reached Anniston, Alabama, a mob slashed the tires of one of the buses, threw a firebomb inside it, and attacked passengers with clubs and bicycle chains as they escaped the burning vehicle. Ku Klux Klan members ambushed riders on the other bus at the bus station in Birmingham. CORE leader James Farmer now had exactly what he wanted: pictures of a burning bus and bloody Freedom Riders in newspapers and on television screens around the world.

A second group of Freedom Riders, including the already injured John Lewis, took up the journey in Nashville, Tennessee. Two days later they arrived in Montgomery, where they were supposed to have been protected by local police. But when a mob met the buses at the Montgomery bus station, the police were nowhere to be seen. Klan members had been assured that they would be given fifteen minutes to release the full force of their rage on the Riders before the police would intervene.

The violence was gruesome and indiscriminate. In the time the police allowed for the attack, reporters were punched, photographers were beaten with their own cameras, and by-standers were pummeled with iron pipes and baseball bats. A gang punched out the teeth of Rider Jim Zwerg. Also attacked was Robert Kennedy's chief assistant at the Justice Department, John Seigenthaler. The Kennedys were no longer observers.

Almost all of the riders, including John Lewis, had

to be hospitalized. Then, after they receiving treatment, they had to be spirited away and hidden from the police, who wanted to arrest them for breaking the segregation laws.

King was in Chicago when news of the attacks reached him. Against the wishes of Robert Kennedy, who wanted to avoid further violence, he flew at once to Montgomery, where a mass meeting at Ralph Abernathy's First Baptist Church was planned for that night. Kennedy sent U.S. marshals to Montgomery to protect King from what looked to be an increasingly volatile situation. These are the men who meet King at the airport.

UNDER SIEGE

ow the congregation files into the First Baptist Church, brushing past a growing crowd of angry whites. Some have driven to Montgomery from elsewhere in the state to threaten the black protesters. Armed with bats, pipes, and chains, they've surrounded the church. A thin line of U.S. marshals stands between the church and the advancing mob. Inside the church, for their own protection, the Freedom Riders are seated apart from each other to avoid easy detection by the local police. They're surrounded by about 1,500 supporters.

King, in a basement office, hears from some late arrivals that the mob outside is two thousand strong and growing. Against the advice of the other leaders, King insists on going outside to assess the situation. "Leadership must do this," he says. As King and several others make a cautious circle around the church, rocks bounce at their feet. When a metal canister lands nearby, they retreat inside. Word comes in that a car has been overturned and set on fire. *How long*, King wonders, *before they set this church on fire?*

From inside the church basement, King is arguing over the telephone with Robert Kennedy. He demands more federal marshals. They're coming, Kennedy says.

"If they [the marshals] don't get here immediately," King says, "we're going to have a bloody confrontation. Because they [the attackers] are at the door now." He can hear the mob pounding on it.

The extra marshals arrive soon afterward and fire volleys of tear gas at the mob, driving it back. Unfortunately, the gas drifts near the marshals themselves and gives the mob a chance to threaten the church again. A brick flies through a church window, then another and another, showering shards of glass over the crowd. The tear gas wafts in.

Rescue finally comes from an unlikely ally. Governor Patterson, giving in to federal demands, sends in the Alabama National Guard troops. The white-helmeted soldiers drive the mob back to a safe distance before it can succeed in burning down the church. At four o'clock in the morning, the exhausted, frightened crowd inside the church finally leaves under protection of the National Guard.

Outside Anniston, Alabama, Freedom Riders have fled from their bus, which has been set on fire.

RIDING LESSONS

The Freedom Rides will continue all summer in 1961, and will result in Attorney General Kennedy taking a stand against segregation in bus stations. The Riders will prove that the federal government can be moved to enforce civil rights when states don't.

To the great disappointment of John Lewis and some of the other Riders, King will not join them. He is on probation after an arrest in an earlier protest, and he doesn't want to risk a long jail term on a technicality. That's not excuse enough for some of them, who will question his courage and his role as a leader. He has been a divine figure for some of them, and they have trouble accepting his normal human qualities.

Still, his respect and support for the Riders is great, and while their tactics are more aggressive than he can personally accept at the moment, the fact that he's one step removed from the Riders makes him a valuable broker in the negotiations with the Kennedy government. He rejects Robert Kennedy's call for a "cooling-off period" and supports the Riders insistence that the Rides continue. Later, when Riders are arrested in Jackson, Mississippi, he supports their refusal of an offer by Robert Kennedy to have them released.

The Freedom Rides begin a new phase in the civil

rights movement. King may seem to have fewer fol-
lowers, but the movement is strengthened by having more leaders, even when they challenge King. He
knows they're all a step closer to their goal. **4**

BIRMINGHAM JAIL

Birmingham, Alabama.

Working in secret, Martin Luther King Jr. is writing the defining statement of the American civil rights movement. What Jefferson's Declaration of Independence was to the American Revolution—a declaration of equality before the law and a warning that injustice would no longer be suffered—the document King is drafting today will be for those Americans the Revolution failed to free.

He's not at his desk at Ebenezer Baptist Church in Atlanta, nor in a comfortable hotel before a speaking engagement. He's sitting alone in a cell at the Birmingham city jail, writing on notebook paper smuggled in by one of his lawyers.

Over the clattering of the trains moving slowly along the nearby railroad tracks, he hears a guard approaching the cell door. He hides his work underneath his shirt, then he casually lies down on the metal slats of the prison bed. *If I had a mattress I could hide a whole book,* he thinks.

His lawyer thinks King *is* writing a whole book. King has written eighteen pages already and seems to have more to say.

What he's writing will become known as the "Letter from Birmingham Jail." It's an answer to eight local white clergymen who have written a public statement criticizing King and the efforts to desegregate Birmingham.

Although King's reply is addressed to those men,

it's meant to be read by the entire nation. He's committing to paper every argument he knows for nonviolent protest in the quest for racial justice.

BITTER ALBANY

King doesn't have to be in jail. Some of the Birmingham authorities would rather he weren't—they look bad for putting him there. As the civil rights movement's most famous figurehead, King draws national attention whenever he goes to jail. But he insists: If they are going to arrest him and charge him with a crime, they'll have to live with the bad publicity.

That insight was something he learned the hard way the previous summer. When he was jailed in Albany, Georgia, the mayor cleverly arranged to have the city pay his fine anonymously. King mistakenly thought a supporter had done it, and he accepted release. King was criticized by people in the civil rights movement for lacking commitment to the cause.

Albany had been a bad experience for other reasons, too. At nearly every turn, the local authorities outmaneuvered the protesters. The police chief, knowing the city was under scrutiny by the media, never resorted to the violence that would normally have occurred. The protesters were duped into postponing demonstrations by the promise of negotiations that never happened. The judge convicted the protesters for disturbing the peace but shrewdly let them off without jail.

When the protest ended, the city remained, in the words of one observer, "a monument to white supremacy."

King and the SCLC vowed to learn from their mistakes. They had failed in Albany because of poor planning. It wouldn't happen in their next effort, in Birmingham, Alabama.

PROJECT C

King considered Birmingham "the most segregated city in America." Its commitment to racism was ridiculous and spiteful. It had gone as far as closing its parks and disbanding its baseball team rather than allow them to be desegregated.

Determined to apply the lessons of Albany to Birmingham, King and his associates planned what they called Project C, for "confrontation." They focused on the downtown business community rather than all the offenders. They set up workshops to teach nonviolent techniques. They learned which locations would be most effective for a protest.

Being outsmarted in Birmingham wasn't likely. The commissioner of public safety (police commissioner), T. E. "Bull" Connor, an extreme racist, had been an embarrassment to the city for years. It wasn't long before Connor's police used dogs and clubs to attack the protesters. Then on April 1 2 King and about fifty other protestors were arrested. King was placed in solitary confinement.

That's where he's been for three days now, writing.

UNWISE AND UNTIMELY

Shortly after being locked up, King saw a newspaper with the clergymen's public statement. It infuriated him. They called the protests "unwise and untimely." They implored blacks to work through negotiation and the court system rather than taking their grievances to the streets. They said that even if the protesters were nonviolent, they were ultimately responsible for the police attacks they suffered. They asked the protesters to ignore "outsiders" like King. "[A] cause should be pressed in the courts . . . not in the streets," they said,

Martin Luther King Jr. sits in a jail cell at the Jefferson County
Courthouse in Birmingham, Alabama.

ignoring the lack of justice for African Americans in the Birmingham courts.

As a final sign of their lack of understanding, they added, "We commend . . . law enforcement officials in particular, on the calm manner in which these demonstrations have been handled."

> JIM CROW LAWS WERE SO EFFECTIVE THAT IN 1940 THERE WAS NOT A SINGLE BLACK JUDGE OR POLICEMAN IN ALABAMA, GEORGIA, LOUISIANA, MISSISSIPPI, OR SOUTH CAROLINA.

King feels betrayed. He is a clergyman. His father is a clergyman. One of his grandfathers was a clergyman. Do these men not understand the clergy's role in helping the poor and oppressed? Do they not understand Jefferson's words in the Declaration of Independence, "all men are created equal . . . endowed by their Creator with certain unalienable rights"? King was arrested on Good Friday, one of the holiest days in the calendar for most of the clergy who signed the letter. Do they fail to recognize the religious parallels to this struggle—to the persecution of Jews in Babylon and Egypt, and of Christians in the Roman Empire? Have they forgotten the protests of early Jews and Christians? *There is nothing new about this kind of civil disobedience*, he thinks.

King, sitting in solitary, immediately starts drafting his reply to the clergymen in the margins of the newspaper containing their statement. At first his colleagues were annoyed that King was not addressing more urgent issues, but now they see the potential power of the document.

"THIS DECISIVE HOUR"

"Law and order exist for the purpose of establishing justice," King writes. If African Americans are not allowed to demonstrate nonviolently, they will eventually choose violence. Civil disobedience isn't disrespectful of the rule of law, he explains. It's not an evasion. It shows "the highest respect for law" as an idea, and simply draws attention to laws that are unjust.

He's also heard enough calls for patience from people who already live comfortable lives. "For years now I have heard the word 'Wait!' " he writes. "It rings in the ear of every Negro with piercing familiarity. This 'Wait' has almost always meant 'Never.' "

King explains to the clergymen—and to their wider audience—facts about African American history that are widely taught today but which were left out of history books at the time: The condition of black America is directly connected to 340 years (at the time) of slavery and servitude, including laws designed specifically to hold back African Americans. In many slave states, for example, it was a crime to teach slaves to read and write. Slave owners were afraid that education was a step toward freedom.

To the claim that the protesters are responsible for the violence inflicted on them, King asks if the man holding money should be blamed for inciting someone to rob him.

He rejects their comments about his being an "outsider." He has a right to fight injustice in Birmingham or anywhere else in the country. More than that, he has a responsibility, one that goes back to the first Christian missionaries, and that they also share. He defiantly tells the clergymen that they're wrong for not joining him: "[T]he judgment of God is upon the church as never before. . . . Is organized religion too inextricably bound to the status quo to save our nation and the world? . . . I am thankful to God that some noble souls from the ranks of organized religion have broken loose from the paralyzing chains of conformity and joined us as active partners in the struggle for freedom. . . . I hope the church as a whole will meet the challenge of this decisive hour."

He's also "profoundly" troubled that the clergymen credit the police with preventing violence rather than creating it. "You warmly commended the Birmingham police force for keeping 'order' and 'preventing violence,'" he writes. "I doubt that you would have so warmly commended the police force if you had seen its dogs sinking their teeth into unarmed, nonviolent Negroes."

The clergymen have it exactly wrong, he tells them. "I wish," he continues, "you had commended the Negro sit-inners and demonstrators of Birmingham for their sublime courage, their willingness to suffer, and their amazing discipline in the midst of great provocation."

King writes the final sentence and slips the papers into his lawyer's briefcase. The seven-thousand-word letter will first be published as a pamphlet, then will appear in a several national magazines. A million copies will be circulated in churches. It will become a chapter in King's book, *Why We Can't Wait*.

Having made his point forcefully, King will accept release from jail so he can continue organizing protests. Project C will continue for almost another month. Children will join the protests, and the country will be shocked by images of them attacked by police dogs and blasted with a high-pressure fire hose. The disgust of the world will then force the city to negotiate with the protesters and give them the rights they should have already enjoyed. It will also force the federal government to increase its support for the protesters. The Supreme Court will declare Birmingham's segregation laws unconstitutional, and shortly afterward President Kennedy will call for Congress to pass a strong civil rights law. In support of this legislation, King and his colleagues will plan the greatest nonviolent demonstration the country has ever seen. The time for waiting is long past. **⑤**

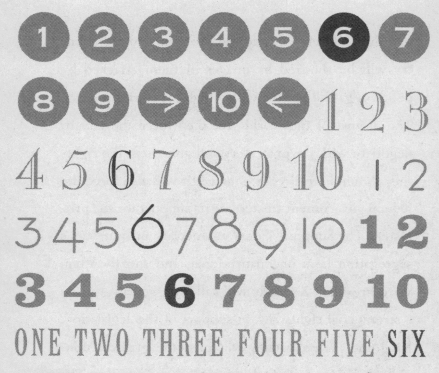

1 2 3 4 5 6 7
8 9 → 10 ←

1 2 3
4 5 6 7 8 9 10 1 2
3 4 5 6 7 8 9 10 12
3 4 5 6 7 8 9 10

ONE TWO THREE FOUR FIVE SIX

DAY ^six

AUGUST 28, 1963

6

A DREAM

Washington, D.C.

A crowd begins to assemble on the lawn of the National Mall not far from the Lincoln Memorial. Martin Luther King Jr. watches from his hotel suite, wondering how many will show up for what he hopes will be the largest demonstration the country has ever seen. He hears a reporter on television estimate the crowd at 25,000, enough to fill New York's Carnegie Hall nine times over. *That's not enough*, he thinks. *Not nearly enough.*

King is hoping that at least 100,000 will assemble here in the nation's capital in what has been named the March on Washington for Jobs and Freedom. The size of the crowd will show Congress how strongly African Americans feel about the civil rights bill that President Kennedy is urging them to pass. Preparations for the march have been going on all summer. The summer has also seen more than seven hundred nonviolent demonstrations in some 186 cities across the South.

THE PRESIDENTIAL SEAL

By this time King and other black leaders understand that President Kennedy is a valuable ally in their cause. In a speech after the movement's victory in Birmingham, the president called on Congress to enact a civil rights bill that would put an end to segregation. King was elated. The president was on his side. But King also had seen the limits of Kennedy's support. Earlier in the summer King and a number of his colleagues met with the president to discuss today's march. Kennedy was against it. He worried that some congressmen wouldn't want to appear to be giving in to pressure, and would vote against the civil rights bill. He also worried that the march might become violent, turning public opinion against the movement and himself.

King and the others stood their ground. The march would happen, they told the president, whether it seemed ill-timed or not. "Some people," King said, "thought Birmingham ill-timed." Reluctantly, Kennedy gave the march his official approval.

EIGHT MINUTES

King knows the march represents something more than just a plea to Congress. Politically, it's an extension of the civil rights movement to all poor people of any color. Symbolically, it's a celebration of the movement's remarkable successes so far, and a display of the breadth and depth of the movement's many strong organizations and charismatic leaders.

At midmorning the numbers are looking better. Reports come in that 90,000 have arrived, with more on the way. Assured that, numerically at least, the march will be a success, King returns to the question of his speech, which he's been trying to prepare for a few days. There are many speakers on the program, and although his speech will be given last, he has only been allotted eight minutes. *What can I possibly say in eight minutes?* he thinks. In the past year King has given an average of almost a speech a day, but never is he confined to a mere eight minutes. In eight minutes he'll just be getting warmed up.

He spent much of last night honing his speech to include the themes he wants to address. It lacks the elaborate oratorical poetry that makes his speeches so inspirational and memorable, but he has so much to say and so little time.

"SCORCHED EARTH"

By noon it's clear that the real numbers will smash all the estimates. It now looks like 250,000 people have come to Washington—almost one-third of them white or Hispanic. They gather on both sides of the long, narrow reflecting pool that faces the Lincoln Memorial. Hollywood stars like Sidney Poitier, Charlton Heston, and Marlon Brando add glamour to the event. Popular folk singers who have embraced the movement, like Joan Baez, Bob Dylan, and Peter, Paul and Mary, sing protest songs. Gospel singer Odetta captivates the gathering with spirituals.

As the list of speakers takes the podium in turn, backstage a battle brews. John Lewis of SNCC, one of the scheduled speakers, has written a speech that some, including President Kennedy, find troubling. Phrases like "the revolution is at hand," "scorched-earth policy," and "we will burn Jim Crow to the ground" sound far too violent. King is worried that it will embarrass Kennedy at the wrong time. Lewis, who's more fiery than King, argues that the civil rights bill that King and Kennedy want to see in place shouldn't be overpraised. All the laws to protect African Americans already exist in the Constitution. What's needed isn't a new one; what's needed is enforcement of the old ones. But Lewis does agree to rewrite parts of his speech, and it's warmly received by the audience.

> THE MARCH WAS THE BRAINCHILD OF A. PHILIP RANDOLPH, FOUNDER OF THE POWERFUL UNION THAT REPRESENTED TRAIN PORTERS. HE AND COLLEAGUES HAD ALSO PLANNED A SIMILAR MARCH IN 1941. IT WAS CANCELLED AFTER PRESIDENT FRANKLIN ROOSEVELT AGREED TO SOME OF THEIR DEMANDS.

By three o'clock in the afternoon, the attention of the massive crowd begins to wander. The speeches have gone on a long time. Fortunately, the singer Mahalia Jackson comes onstage. As cameras of all three major television networks beam live images of her and the crowd to every corner of the nation, Jackson electrifies the crowd.

A little after she's done, King is introduced as "the moral leader of the nation." He's certainly the person the marchers have come to hear.

"I HAVE A DREAM"

His opening words echo those of Abraham Lincoln's Gettysburg Address. "Five score years ago, a great American, in whose symbolic shadow we stand today, signed the Emancipation Proclamation. This momentous decree came as a great beacon light of hope to millions of

Negro slaves who had been seared in the flames of withering injustice. It came as a joyous daybreak to end the long night of their captivity. But one hundred years later, the Negro is still not free."

King delivers his speech as he wrote it the night before. He talks about the promise of freedom that blacks have so far been denied—freedoms they have come here to demand. "We have also come to this hallowed spot," he says "to remind America of the fierce urgency of now. . . . Now is the time to make justice a reality for all of God's children."

He warns the nation that peace will not come to America until there is justice for all. Then he warns blacks to avoid bitterness and hatred. He implores them to remain nonviolent and to embrace the sympathetic whites who have willingly joined their struggle.

He answers those who ask of blacks, "When will you be satisfied?" Never, he says, as long as blacks are victims of police brutality, segregation, and humiliation, and as long as they are denied the right to vote.

The view of the National Mall from the stage at the Lincoln Memorial. The Reflecting Pool and the Washington Monument are in the background.

It's a good speech, but something's missing. He knows it. He can sense he hasn't reached the crowd as he'd hoped.

Mahalia Jackson, still on stage, can sense it too. She knows what's missing. King is aiming at their minds. He wants the marchers, and maybe even more important, the people watching at home, to understand the reasons for the movement: its basis in philosophy, the rule of law, and the history and economics of the country. Jackson knows King needs to aim at their hearts instead.

She calls out to him, "Tell 'em about the dream, Martin."

The dream. The promised land. The freedom and equality that was promised in the Declaration of Independence and the Constitution of the United States and even the Bible, and that is the single, overarching idea that has brought together here in Washington a quarter of a million people from every background. Tell 'em about *the dream.*

He does, and the crowd is spellbound.

I say to you today, my friends: So even though we face the difficulties of today and tomorrow, I still have a dream."

Equality. Justice. Freedom. "I have a dream," he repeats again and again, painting the details of a glowing, inspirational picture of an America freed from the stain of prejudice and hatred, where people "will not be judged by the color of their skin but by the content of their character."

This dream, he reminds the crowd, is the founding ideal of America, expressed in the Declaration of Independence, the civil rights protest of the Founding Fathers: "All men are created equal." For King, these aren't just Thomas Jefferson's words. They're God's law. The strong religious foundations of his belief leave no doubts for him: The salvation of all Americans lies in casting aside the evil of racial hate. Racism is a tragedy for the victim and a sin for the oppressor.

This, he tells the crowd, is his dream: the day when "all of God's children, black men and white men, Jews and Gentiles, Protestants and Catholics, will be able to join hands and sing in the words of the old Negro spiritual, 'Free at last! Free at last! Thank God Almighty, we are free at last!'" **6**

① ② ③ ④ ⑤ ⑥ ⑦

⑧ ⑨ → ⑩ ← 1 2 3

4 5 6 7 8 9 10 1 2

3 4 5 6 7 8 9 10 **1 2**

3 4 5 6 7 8 9 10

ONE TWO THREE FOUR FIVE SIX

DAY SEVEN 7

DECEMBER 10,
1964 7

EYES ON THE PRIZE

Oslo, Norway.

It has been a roller coaster of a year for King, and this moment is no different.

Right now, he's heading toward a pinnacle: the exhilaration that comes with winning the most prestigious honor on earth, the Nobel Peace Prize, which he'll be awarded this evening at a ceremony in Oslo. At just thirty-five years old, he'll be the youngest person ever to receive it.

But King knows that a stomach-churning drop is

soon to follow: He has learned that J. Edgar Hoover, the head of the Federal Bureau of Investigation, is determined to ruin King's reputation and end his role in the civil rights movement. King made some legitimate criticisms of the FBI, which had not vigorously pursued the segregationists and white supremacists behind some of the violence against African Americans. Hoover, who has been distrustful of King for almost a decade and has ordered many investigations of him, several of them illegal, held a rare and bizarre press conference in which he brushed aside King's claims by calling King "the most notorious liar in the country." Privately, Hoover has threatened worse. William Sullivan, the head of the FBI's spying operations, wrote to Hoover two days after the March on Washington that "We must mark [King] now, if we have not done so before, as the most dangerous Negro of the future in this nation from the standpoint of communism, the Negro, and national security. . . ." More recently—about three weeks before this day of the prize ceremony—Sullivan took an astonishing step. He wrote and typed, on an untraceable typewriter, an anonymous threatening letter to King that was meant to sound as if it came from an angry African American:

> King,
>
> In view of your low grade . . . I will not dignify your name with either a Mr. or a Reverend or a Dr. And, your last name calls to mind only the type of king such as King Henry the VIII. . . .
>
> King, look into your heart. You know you are a complete my fraud and great liability to all of us Negroes. White people in this country have enough frauds of their own but I am sure they don't have one at this time that is anywhere near your equal. You are no clergyman and you know it. I repeat you are a colossal fraud and an evil, vicious one at that. You could not believe in God . . . Clearly you don't believe in any personal moral principles.

King, like all frauds, your end is approaching.
You could have been our greatest leader. You, even
at an early age have turned out to be not a leader
but a dissolute, abnormal moral imbecile. We will
now have to depend on our older leaders like
Wilkins[,] a man of character[,] and thank God
we have others like him. But you are done. Your
"honorary" degrees, your Nobel Prize (what a grim
farce) and other awards will not save you. King, I
repeat, you are done.

No person can overcome facts, not even a
fraud like yourself . . . I repeat—no person can
argue successfully against facts. You are fin-
ished. . . . Satan could not do more. What incred-
ible evilness. . . . King you are done.

The American public, the church organizations
that have been helping—Protestant, Catholic
and Jews will know you for what you are—an
evil, abnormal beast. So will others who have
backed you. You are done.

King, there is only one thing left for you to do. You know what it is. You have just 34 days in which to do (this exact number has been selected for a specific reason, it has definite practical significant [sic].) You are done. There is but one way out for you. You better take it before your filthy, abnormal fraudulent self is bared to the nation.

Along with the letter Sullivan will send an audiotape the FBI had made by planting spy microphones in King's hotel rooms. On the tape are recordings of King with women other than his wife, Coretta. The FBI believes this threat will lead King to commit suicide. It's a bizarre, absurd, and shameful effort by a powerful government agency that should have been protecting the protest movement instead of trying to undermine it with childish tricks.

Adding to the tension of this day in Oslo, King is unable to turn to the man he usually relies upon for support. The Reverend Ralph Abernathy of the First

Baptist Church in Montgomery, his close colleague since the days of the first bus boycott, is resentful that King is being singled out for the Nobel Prize. Here in Oslo, Abernathy's behavior has been petulant.

On this day of international recognition and honor, King is feeling very much alone.

UNEASY LIES THE HEAD

This dark mood has been a long time coming. The assassination of President Kennedy, just over a year ago, was a stunning blow. King had seen Kennedy grow from a cautious politician, reluctant to upset Southern whites, to a champion of the civil rights movement. Then suddenly Kennedy was gone. Every American felt something; but few could understand what it meant to be at risk of assassination every day. King could. "This," he said to Coretta, "is what is going to happen to me."

The family of the slain president did not invite King to the funeral. He went to Washington anyway and stood anonymously on the sidewalk as the funeral procession rolled slowly by. The idea of his premature death—of assassination—had begun to take hold.

As a result, he pushed himself to work harder and accomplish more. His first concern was the civil rights bill that Kennedy had proposed to Congress. He wondered whether the new president, Lyndon Johnson, would support it or allow it to die. As a legislator, Johnson had voted against civil rights legislation. But in a meeting at the White House, Johnson assured him that "John Kennedy's dream of equality [had] not died with him," and swore to use "every ounce of strength I [possess] to gain justice for the black American."

King hoped that was true. It wasn't something anyone expected from Johnson, who had the reputation of a being pragmatic, deal-making politician, not a man driven by a cause.

King and his SCLC colleagues immediately looked

for another segregated city where they might repeat the integration success of Birmingham. They wanted to keep up the pressure on Johnson and Congress. They chose St. Augustine, Florida, the oldest city in America, which was preparing to celebrate its four-hundredth anniversary. Much of St. Augustine's economy depended on tourism, which meant the city government would be sensitive to bad publicity. That would be good for the protesters.

What they didn't count on was the city's lack of control over the local Ku Klux Klan. The Klan was free, as one of its members put it, to commit violence "anytime, anyplace, anywhere." On one particularly horrific night of the protest, a mob of eight hundred whites assaulted marchers with trash cans, park benches, tire tools, and chains. The Klan also threatened business owners with violence if they agreed to the SCLC's demands. But the ferocity of white violence in St. Augustine helped convince Congress to pass the Civil Rights Act.

GLORY DAYS

King was in a hospital, being treated for exhaustion caused by his nonstop schedule, when he learned about the Nobel Prize. He was both ecstatic and humbled. He had always felt some guilt about the attention he received. He had grown up in a privileged home with a fine education and material comfort. He had never suffered in the way that millions of others in the civil rights movement had done. To underscore the idea that the award did not belong to him personally, he donated all of the $54,000 prize money to the SCLC and other civil rights organizations, despite Coretta's request that he set aside some of it for their children's education.

Now, this evening in Oslo, wearing the traditional striped trousers and gray tailcoat worn at the Nobel Prize ceremony, King accepts the gold medallion on behalf of the entire civil rights movement. He explains the award as recognition for the method

Keystone/Getty Images

King receives the Nobel Prize for Peace from Gunnar Jahn,
president of the Nobel Prize Committee.

of nonviolence, "a powerful moral force" and the "answer to the crucial political and moral questions of our time—the need for man to overcome oppression and violence without resorting to violence and oppression."

"DO THE RIGHT THING"

After his triumphant trip to Oslo, King will be invited to meet with President Johnson. They will discuss a voting rights bill, which King will argue is crucial if blacks are ever to achieve real equality in the South. Johnson tells King it will be difficult to pass a bill so soon after the Civil Rights Act. However, he'll slyly encourage King to use nonviolent demonstrations to spur government action. "Now, Dr. King," he will say, "you go out there and make it possible for me to do the right thing."

King will accept that presidential challenge and wage what will, unfortunately, turn out to be his last great campaign. **7**

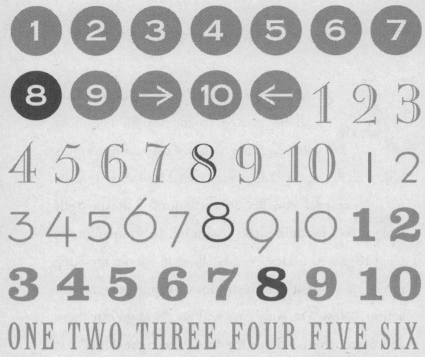

ONE TWO THREE FOUR FIVE SIX

DAY **8**

8

MARCH 15,

1965

EIGHT

"THIS IS SELMA"

Selma, Alabama.

There are 15,000 African American citizens in and around Selma, more than half the town's total population. But only 130 are registered to vote.

The white authorities of Alabama go to a lot of trouble to prevent African Americans from voting. Registration offices are open just a few hours a month. Anyone with a job must ask for time off from work; any employer who might give permission would know that the authorities and local vigilante groups will create problems for the business. Getting to the office doesn't guarantee registration. A local sheriff will be there with a phony reason to deny entry. If the applicant gets inside, the next step is a "literacy test" with difficult and confusing questions.

For example, "Name one area of authority over state militia reserved exclusively to the states." (Answer: "The appointment of officers.") Forget about memorizing the answers, because more than a hundred different tests exist. What's more, the answers don't matter. A committee reviews the test, which can be rejected for any reason. The committee may not even meet for several months.

Of course, whites don't face the same difficulties. In 1900, Alabama said that anyone descended from a previous voter didn't have to take the test, nor did "all who are of good character and understand the duties and obligations of citizenship." The legislators who created the law meant it to exclude only black voters, and that's how it has been enforced. The federal government, fearful of losing support of Southern voters, has never intruded.

Fortunately, things are about to change this day. The reason will be a surprise for the entire nation, and no one will be more surprised than King.

THIS IS SELMA

The Student Nonviolent Coordinating Committee (SNCC) has been patiently at work in Selma for two years. When King wanted his SCLC to begin a voting-rights drive, Selma looked like a good choice.

However, the two groups were wary of each other. The passionate young people of SNCC worried that the SCLC was becoming too willing to compromise with white authorities and to accept smaller victories than were possible. But differences were put aside and they agreed upon a plan.

King and his colleagues expected that the county sheriff, Jim Clark, who has never hidden his hostility to African Americans, would quickly react to a protest with such violence that the nation would take notice. They were right. Clark knew he should try to restrain himself, especially with so many reporters in Selma, but he couldn't. He personally dragged one female protester half a block by her hair, and struck another, a woman in her fifties, on the head with his billy club.

He also did nothing to stop the many counter-protesters who had come to Selma: the Ku Klux Klan, of course, and also members of the American Nazi Party and the similarly minded National States Rights Party. A member of the NSRP got close enough to King to punch him in the face. One of the Nazi Party members, Robert Lloyd, dressed as a minstrel and wore blackface. His lunacy was too much even for the local authorities, who threw him in jail to keep him off the streets.

Clark and the local authorities tried to control the

protesters by forcing them to remain in a small area near the Brown Chapel, which had become the center of the protest. But that simply meant that nearly any action was an illegal action, and he had to respond to it or give ground. It wasn't long before King himself was in jail. King and his colleagues had essentially planned the arrest, and they had prepared a letter from King to be placed as an advertisement in the *New York Times*: "When the King of Norway participated in awarding the Nobel Peace Prize to me he surely did not expect that in less than sixty days I would be in jail. . . . This is Selma, Alabama. There are more Negroes in jail with me than there are on the voting rolls."

The protesters were changing minds in many parts of America, and even the rest of the world; but they were still struggling to change the minds of white Alabamans. The segregationist governor of the state, George Wallace, had no sympathy at all for blacks who wanted to vote.

Moderates in Alabama—that's to say, those whites who didn't mind if African Americans got the vote, but who weren't going to do much about it, and really just wanted the problem to go away—were becoming uncomfortable with the attention Selma and the state were receiving. They were also beginning to fear that the protests would become violent. Part of that worry came from the numbers: In some towns whites were the minority.

While King sat in jail, a very different civil rights leader visited Selma. Malcolm X, an influential, charismatic black leader, had in the past ridiculed King's method of nonviolent resistance. He offered a vision of equality for blacks wrested from white power with brute force, if necessary. But Malcolm X, like King an intelligent tactician, knew that his reputation was useful. After speaking at a rally, he said to Coretta King, "I want Dr. King to know that I didn't come to Selma to make his job difficult," Malcolm said. "I really did come thinking that I could make it easier. If the white people realize what the alternative is, perhaps they will be more willing to hear Dr. King."

BLOODY SUNDAY

Then from tragedy came inspiration. Troopers attacked protesters in a nearby town and shot a young man who was trying to protect his mother. Civil rights workers visited the man's family and were so moved they vowed to march from Selma to Montgomery, about fifty miles, to symbolically confront Governor George Wallace with facts about the young man's death.

The march began at the Brown Chapel and headed directly for the Edmund Pettus Bridge, named after a Confederate general. Worried by death threats, King's colleagues convinced him to stay in Atlanta that day. Instead, John Lewis of SNCC and Hosea Williams of the SCLC, two leaders known for their bravery, led the five hundred or so marchers. Williams had been beaten many times for individual and group protests. Lewis had been abused and beaten at student sit-ins and as a Freedom Rider.

Across the bridge from the marchers stood a line of state troopers, ordered by Governor Wallace. They were backed up by Sheriff Clark's men. Newspaper reporters and television cameras took positions nearby to record the unfolding drama.

Lewis and Williams were given two minutes to turn around and return to the church. They stood their ground. At a signal, the troopers put on gas masks and advanced, on foot and on horseback, over-whelming the marchers with nightsticks, cattle prods, bullwhips, and tear gas. The marchers were chased back over the bridge and into the church. More than a hundred sustained injuries. Lewis was clubbed so hard his skull was fractured. He later said, "I don't know from that day to this how I made it back to the church."

Television cameras captured the entire episode, which came to be known as Bloody Sunday. The three major networks interrupted their Sunday night programming to show footage of the brutality. Viewers across the country were horrified by the troopers' actions.

King rushed back to Selma and called for another march. He regretted his decision not to lead the first, and he would lead the second. He issued a national call for clergymen to join him. Then a federal court issued an order to halt the second march.

Hosea Williams, left, and John Lewis lead the marchers across the Edmund Pettus Bridge while a helmeted trooper watches.

King had never defied a federal court, whose rulings usually proved beneficial to the movement. Fearing a loss of confidence if he didn't march, he settled on an awkward compromise, arranged in advance with federal officials. King led two thousand marchers to the spot where the first march had been halted. There, they knelt in prayer before King turned them around and headed back to the church.

Some of King's colleagues felt betrayed. But the squabbling ended that evening when a clergymen who had come to Selma to march, a Unitarian minister from Boston named James Reeb, was clubbed unconscious by white racists. He died two days later.

President Johnson has had enough. He's already warned Governor Wallace to change Alabama's policies. Since that hasn't worked, Johnson will now move boldly to solve the problem. He's going to make a special appearance before Congress, to be televised live during the family viewing hours of the evening, announcing his decision to send a voting rights bill to Congress. It has been nineteen years since a president has given a special address to Congress on a subject other than war.

Johnson invites King to be a guest at the speech, but King has to decline so he can speak at the funeral service for Reverend Reeb.

OVERCOME

Now this evening, following the service, King and some of his colleagues are at the home of a supporter to watch and listen to the president. King wonders if the president will be cautious because of the large audience. He knows that the support he receives privately from politicians can disappear in public moments.

Then Johnson begins the address:

At times history and fate meet at a single time in a single place to shape a turning point in man's

unending search for freedom. So it was at Lexington
and Concord. So it was a century ago at Appomattox.
So it was last week in Selma, Alabama.

King and his colleagues are awestruck. President
Johnson has just equated the Selma protesters with the
colonists who started the American revolution.

Johnson continues:

> *. . . [T]he harsh fact is that in many places in*
> *this country men and women are kept from voting*
> *simply because they are Negroes.*
>
> *Every device of which human ingenuity is ca-*
> *pable has been used to deny this right.*

After telling the public in detail about the
hurdles local authorities have put in the way of
voting—the unavailable registrars, the tests that can't
be passed, the harassment of any African American
who tries—Johnson speaks to America bluntly:

For the fact is that the only way to pass these bar-
riers is to show a white skin.

. . . No law that we now have on the books—
and I have helped to put three of them there—
can ensure the right to vote when local officials
are determined to deny it.

. . .Wednesday I will send to Congress a law de-
signed to eliminate illegal barriers to the right to
vote. . . . This bill will strike down restrictions to voting
in all elections—federal, state, and local—which
have been used to deny Negroes the right to vote.

King feels as if a weight has been lifted from his shoulders. The untold sacrifice by thousands who have endured beatings, bombings, hosings, dogs, and tear gas has finally been rewarded. The president has taken up their cause, and he is putting the full power of his office behind the movement.

Then King is stunned by what he hears from the President:

. . . [I]t is not just Negroes, but really it is all of us, who must overcome the crippling legacy of bigotry and injustice.

And we shall overcome.

. . . This great, rich, restless country can offer opportunity and education and hope to all: black and white, North and South, sharecropper and city dweller. These are the enemies: poverty, ignorance, disease. They are the enemies and not our fellow man, not our neighbor. And these enemies too, poverty, disease and ignorance, we shall overcome.

We shall overcome. King has just heard the president of the United States use the very words that have come to symbolize the movement——*his* words. A tear rolls down his cheek. It's the first time his associates have ever seen him cry.

John Lewis would later call Johnson's address "probably the strongest speech any American president has ever made on the subject of civil rights."

Within a week, King will lead 3,200 protesters, clergymen, maids, nuns, movie stars, and students—protected by 3,000 federal troops and two helicopters—in a victorious procession across the bridge and down the highway to Montgomery.

A few months later Congress will pass the Voting Rights Act. ⑧

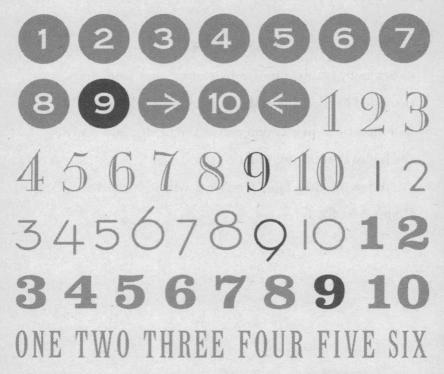

ONE TWO THREE FOUR FIVE SIX

DAY

NINE
9

JUNE 26,
1966

9

MARCH AGAINST FEAR

Jackson, Mississippi.

"Black power!"

King winces as he hears the shout from Stokely Carmichael, the new chairman of the SNCC. Carmichael, just a few days away from his twenty-fifth birthday, is speaking to a crowd of maybe fifteen thousand people near the state capitol building. For almost three weeks King and Carmichael, along with several other civil rights leaders and many thousand supporters, have been marching through Mississippi. Though they are marching together, Carmichael has challenged King's belief in an integrated society—what King reverently calls a "beloved community." Carmichael believes that African Americans must self-segregate to survive and thrive. He believes African Americans will gain full constitutional rights only by taking power from the white establishment, either by force or the threat of it. King, who is thirty-seven, is considered out of date by Carmichael and other young protesters.

Integration versus self-segregation. Force versus nonviolent action. These philosophical debates go back to ancient times. Carmichael is not the first in the African American civil rights movement to express his views. They're close to the ideas expressed by Malcolm X, and they arose even earlier: In the late 1800s and early 1900s, many African Americans took steps to move to Africa as a way of separating themselves from the white establishment in America.

Neither side can claim to be right in every case.

Nonviolent noncooperation worked in India to remove British rule; but just a few years earlier it had failed to stop anti-Jewish laws in Nazi Germany.

Assimilation (cultural integration) hadn't worked for German Jews, either. They hadn't been truly accepted—just as Carmichael believes African Americans will never be truly accepted by white Americans.

> MALCOLM X WAS ASSASSINATED IN FEBRUARY 1965 BY MEMBERS OF HIS FORMER RELIGIOUS ORGANIZATION, THE NATION OF ISLAM.

However, King could argue that real progress is being made by nonviolent direction, helped along by many white Americans who detest Jim Crow and segregation and racism.

It's probably more accurate to say that each side in the debate makes the other possible. For the civil rights movement to be successful, a lot of minds have to be changed in white America. A single argument won't work on everyone.

King knows this. What worries him is the balance of opinion within the movement. John Lewis, the previous chairman of the SNCC, shared King's ideals, even when he expressed impatience with King's negotiations with leaders in Washington. But he was moved aside for Carmichael by people who weren't as committed to integration and cooperation and non-violence. Carmichael's backers preferred an exclusively African American effort to take power.

ONE-MAN BAND

Despite their differences, on this day King and Carmichael are here to support and celebrate a lone protester who seems to embody the conflicting philosophies within the movement.

The man at the center of today's demonstration is James Meredith. The march through Mississippi began as his idea. More than that, it began as a one-man march.

Meredith had already earned prominence in the civil rights movement with his efforts to attend the University of Mississippi in 1961. After a legal battle that lasted eighteen months, the court had ordered the university to admit Meredith, but it took more than one hundred U.S. marshals and a bloody, night-long riot before he was quietly registered. In 1963 Meredith became the first African American to graduate from the university.

Meredith's latest effort, the march from Memphis, Tennessee to Jackson, Mississippi, began three weeks before this day. It was meant to encourage blacks to register to vote. But just two days into his march, a man named Aubrey James Norvell, hiding in the brush along the march route, ambushed Meredith and blasted him with a shotgun. Fortunately, Meredith wasn't critically wounded. But he's still confined to a hospital bed.

King, Carmichael, and other leaders of the movement have all visited Meredith in the hospital to offer their support. They want to stage a mass protest.

Meredith rejects this idea and insists he just wants to continue his march. Out of respect, the civil rights leaders agree. During the meeting King notices that Meredith veers more to Carmichael's philosophy than King's. That will soon become even more evident.

James Meredith walks to class at the University of Mississippi in 1962, accompanied by federal marshals, some of them in helmets.

"WE SHALL OVERRUN"

Unlike King, who has always approached the civil rights movement as a Christian ministry, Carmichael comes to it as a student of politics. After graduating from the competitive Bronx High School of Science in New York City, one of the very best schools in the country, he attended Howard University in Washington, D.C., and graduated with a degree in philosophy. He was greatly influenced by academics who combined careful study of colonialism in Africa with a call for the overthrow of the European colonial powers there. The success of many independence movements in sub-Saharan Africa in the early 1960s seemed to Carmichael to prove the value of using force to back up a demand for rights.

The model of colonial Africa also influenced Carmichael's attitude toward white Americans who were working for SNCC. Carmichael didn't believe whites should be allowed in the group. This was a great difference between him and the man he replaced, John Lewis, as well as between him and King.

Soon after King and Carmichael and the others restarted Meredith's march, King noticed that many of the marchers shared Carmichael's views. "This should be an all-black march," he later remembered hearing. "We don't need any more white phonies and liberals invading our movement. This is our march."

When the marchers sang "We Shall Overcome," some refused to sing the words "black and white together." Instead of the words "We shall overcome," they sang, "We shall overrun." As Carmichael explains to King, "Power is the only thing respected in this world, and we must get it at any cost."

Ten days before this protest in Jackson, when the march was in the town of Greenwood, Carmichael had first used the phrase "black power" to rally the marchers. He'd been arrested earlier that day on a made-up charge of "trespassing," and was released with barely enough time to make it to that evening's demonstration. "Every courthouse in Mississippi should be burnt down tomorrow," he told the crowd. "We want black power!" he called out. The audience response came back: "We want black power!"

King thought the phrase was too confrontational. Carmichael and others thought it was just confrontational enough. Meanwhile the marchers were reaching towns even worse than Greenwood. In Philadelphia, Mississippi, where two years earlier three civil rights workers had been murdered, a mob of three hundred whites followed the marchers and threatened them.

"I believe in my heart that the murderers are somewhere around me at this moment," King announced during a memorial service for the murder victims. Chief Deputy Sheriff Cecil Ray Price, standing a few steps behind him, said in a stage whisper King could hear, "You're damn right, they're right behind you now."

A few days later, when the march was in Yazoo City, organizers learned that back in Philadelphia the town's black residents had been attacked. "In Mississippi murder is a popular pastime," King told the crowd. But they should not give in to the natural urge for revenge, or even the calls for self-segregation: "We are ten percent of the population of this nation and it would be foolish for me to stand up and tell you we are going to get our freedom by ourselves," he says. What's necessary, he declares, is for every white American to realize "that segregation denigrates him as much as it does the Negro."

That night the strain he felt was obvious. "I'm sick and tired of violence," he told the crowd. "I'm tired of shooting. I'm tired of hatred. I'm tired of selfishness. I'm tired of evil. I'm not going to use violence, no matter who says it."

THE DESCENDING SPIRAL

Now, a few days later, the march has reached Jackson, its destination, for a mass rally. James Meredith has rejoined it. He's as independent as ever—yesterday morning he set out alone to finish the march the way he began it. And some of the march organizers had to quickly follow after him so reporters wouldn't think he was abandoning the mass protest. It took most of the day for him to be convinced to finish the march with everyone else.

This morning, Meredith is firmly on the side of Carmichael and those in the crowd calling for black power. He shakes a walking stick at some of the speakers who offer a softer message.

"I don't know what I'm going to do," King said to one reporter. "The government has got to give me some victories if I'm going to keep people nonviolent. I know I'm going to stay nonviolent no matter what happens, but a lot of people are getting hurt and bitter, and they can't see it that way anymore."

Later King would described his objection to violence this way: "The ultimate weakness of violence is that it is a descending spiral, begetting the very thing it seeks to destroy. Instead of diminishing evil, it multiplies it. Through violence you may murder the liar, but you cannot murder the lie, nor establish the truth. Through violence you may murder the hater, but you do not murder hate. In fact, violence merely increases hate. So it goes. . . . Returning hate for hate multiplies hate, adding deeper darkness to a night already devoid of stars. Darkness cannot drive out darkness: only light can do that. Hate cannot drive out hate: only love can do that."

But the mood of the civil rights movement is swinging like a pendulum away from King's beliefs. When James Meredith called his protest the "March Against Fear," he was referring to the fear African Americans felt living in a country where they were denied rights at the most basic protection of the law. King feels a different kind of fear. He is afraid the divisions within the movement will weaken it; he is afraid that African American anger, despite being legitimate, will be expressed in violence that will slow the cause of civil rights or possibly reverse the progress that has been made; and he is afraid that his vision of an integrated society, a "beloved community," will be impossible to realize. **9**

① ② ③ ④ ⑤ ⑥ ⑦

⑧ ⑨ → ⑩ ← 1 2 3

4 5 6 7 8 9 10 1 2

3 4 5 6 7 8 9 10 **12**

3 4 5 6 7 8 9 10

ONE TWO THREE FOUR FIVE SIX

DAY 10

APRIL 3,
1968

T
E
N

THE MOUNTAINTOP

Memphis, Tennessee.

A tremendous rainstorm is battering Memphis, and tornado warnings have been issued. King, exhausted from constant traveling, doesn't want to leave his motel. Ralph Abernathy insists King must keep his word to speak to a rally of city sanitation workers. The workers, nearly all of them black, are on strike for better salaries and working conditions following the recent deaths of two of their members in a storm like this one.

King fears the threatening weather will keep the crowd small, and reporters will then blame him personally, calling it a sign that his philosophy of nonviolence is no longer important within the civil rights movement. This negative thinking has become a reflex in the past year. King has become more depressed by the divisions within the movement; by certain people within it who seem to have selfish motives; by the difficulties of integrating the movement so it includes other people of color; and, most important by far, by the arguments that nonviolence isn't working well enough or quickly enough.

King has become a victim of his own success. He always wanted a large community of intelligent, passionate members who would choose the movement's course together. He has that now; and with it he has many colleagues who disagree with him and with each other. He also has people who have joined the movement because its record of successes gives them a chance to fulfill personal ambitions. These unfortunate developments are common when organizations grow, whether in politics or business or even schools. But rather than observe the tensions from a distance, King feels responsible for what he perceives to be the failings of the group.

King has become isolated from his colleagues and his friends. To some extent, that isolation is self-imposed. Unwilling to accept anything other than the philosophy of nonviolent noncooperation that is so important to him, he's withdrawing himself from the movement. But that isolation also comes from being pushed away from colleagues and contacts with whom he once worked closely.

As soon as he became successful in getting the politicians like President Kennedy and President Johnson to listen to the movement's concern, and began to negotiate with them the way forward, he was criticized within the movement by some colleagues who felt he gave away too much. Meanwhile, politicians have grown frustrated that the movement keeps making demands, and that it doesn't act in the predictable manner they'd like. In acting as a diplomat, he has absorbed the hard feelings each side feels for the other.

President Johnson is angry at King for a more specific, concrete reason. King has dared to criticize the growing American military involvement in Vietnam. It will be years before the majority of Americans see the problems King sees with that war. Even some of his colleagues see the issue as minor compared to civil rights. But, as a Nobel Peace Prize laureate, King feels compelled to speak out against a war he believes is morally wrong. "I am mandated by this calling above every other duty," he said, "to seek peace among men and do it even in the face of hysteria and scorn."

But of course King's friends and colleagues have not rejected him personally. They're distressed by the changes in his mood. Worst are the many comments he makes about being assassinated. He refers to this possibility—in his opinion, this inevitability—more and more often. Everyone who works with him knows this risk has always been real, but they also feel King is becoming fixated on the idea, beyond reality.

On this day, they're wrong. A block away from King's room at the Lorraine Motel, an escaped convict named James Earl Ray pays for a room at a boarding house. In his luggage is a high-powered rifle.

THE POOR PEOPLE'S CAMPAIGN

King wonders why he's in Memphis in the first place. While the sanitation workers' strike is important, King isn't one of the organizers. His SCLC is trying to put together a large protest in Washington, D.C., and he needs to give that effort his full attention.

King has begun to consider the issues surrounding oppressed people in global terms. He conceived his next great campaign as a movement to end poverty not just for blacks, but for Hispanics, Native Americans, and even impoverished whites.

The Poor People's Campaign, as he called it, would begin with a massive demonstration in Washington. It would be designed to disrupt the nation's capital and convince Congress to pass an Economic Bill of Rights that would guarantee a job for everyone able to work and an annual income for everyone who couldn't.

A government commission had studied just such a plan, one that would have included decent housing for the poor. The price tag: $32 billion—the cost of waging war in Vietnam for one year. President Johnson, who once hoped to make the elimination of poverty his administration's grandest achievement, rejected the plan as too expensive.

The Poor People's Campaign promised to be the most ambitious, most complicated, and costliest operation ever undertaken by King and the SCLC. Many of his associates thought it too big. They worried whether the participants could be trusted to remain nonviolent. They were having trouble finding grass-roots supporters who would commit to it. King needs all of his energies and persuasive powers to convince them it's the right thing to do.

What has happened so far in Memphis hasn't helped. A few weeks earlier, after a successful speech, King agreed to return to Memphis to lead a protest march. The march was a disaster. The SCLC made none of the usual preparations, instructed no one in the nonviolent philosophy. As King led the way, a number of marchers behind him began breaking store windows and looting. King's colleagues, seeing the march dissolve into a riot, whisked him away to a nearby hotel.

King was in despair. He expected news reporters to criticize the violence, and to question whether the same would occur in Washington if the Poor People's Campaign took place. "Nonviolence as a concept," he told his associates, "is now on trial."

"I MAY NOT GET THERE"

After arguing with Abernathy about appearing at this evening's rally, King finally gives in and rides to its site, the Masonic Temple, through the wind and rain. Once there, he delivers a powerful message, saluting the sanitation workers in their struggle against poverty. Then he offers a prophetic confession of the fears that are consuming him: "We've got some difficult days ahead. But it really doesn't matter with me now. Because I've been to the mountaintop. And I don't mind. Like anybody, I would like to live a long life. Longevity has its place. But I'm not concerned about that now. I just want to do God's will. And he's allowed me to go to the mountain. And I've looked over. And I've seen the promised land. I may not get there with you. But I want you to know tonight, that we, as a people will to get to the promised land." He collapses into Abernathy's arms, spent but elated at the thunderous ovation.

It is hours before he finds his way back to the Lorraine Motel and sleeps. The next day will be his last. When he steps onto the motel balcony to chat with associates in the courtyard below, James Earl Ray will fire a single shot that strikes King in the neck. King will be rushed to a hospital, but will be declared dead one hour later.

Ray will escape at first, traveling as far as Canada and then London, but two months later the FBI will catch him, and, except for a three-day escape, he will spend the rest of his life in prison.

King's assassination will unleash a torrent of grief and rage. Riots will explode in 110 American cities. In Washington alone, 711 fires will be set ablaze, and ten people will die. The *New York Times* will call King's murder "a national disaster, depriving Negroes and whites of a leader of integrity, vision and restraint." *The Times* of London will say that King's death is "a loss to the whole world."

Within two weeks, the mayor of Memphis will

April 4, 1968: Moments after King collapses, others on the balcony of the Lorraine Motel point in the direction of the gunfire so people in the courtyard below can find the assassin.

come to an agreement with the sanitation workers, and Congress will pass the Civil Rights Act of 1968, which bars discrimination in housing.

At his funeral procession, King's coffin will be transported on a farm cart pulled by two mules, symbolizing King's last unfinished dream, the Poor

People's Campaign. The monument on his grave will bear a slightly amended version of the closing from his famous speech in Washington: "Free at last! Free at last! Thank God Almighty I am free at last!" **❿**

1 2 3 4 5 6 7

8 9 → 10 ← 1 2 3

4 5 6 7 8 9 10 1 2

3 4 5 6 7 8 9 10 **12**

3 4 5 6 7 8 9 10

ONE TWO THREE FOUR FIVE SIX

AFTERWORD

NOVEMBER 2,

1983

A DAY TO REMEMBER

Washington, D.C.

On a sunny and crisp Washington morning, President Ronald Reagan stands in the Rose Garden of the White House, with Coretta Scott King and other guests, and reads from a teleprompter the generous remarks about Martin Luther King Jr. that an aide has written. Today President Reagan is signing a bill passed by Congress to establish a national holiday in honor of the slain civil rights leader.

Reagan is gracious in defeat—because defeat is what this bill represents. He's one of many politicians who didn't want to create this holiday. Some have explained it away as a problem for business—a lost day of work would be bad for companies and bad for the economy. That's the polite thing to say.

In fact, animosity toward King lasted long after his death. Opposition to this holiday came from the same places, and in many cases the same people, as opposition to King's work. Senator Jesse Helms of North Carolina, a lifelong opponent of equal rights for African Americans, blocked business in the Senate by orchestrating a filibuster (a nonstop speech) that lasted sixteen days. The state of South Carolina was against it, and for the first fourteen years of the King holiday allowed state employees to take a holiday on days that honored Confederate Army generals instead. Virginia did something similar, combining the holiday with an existing holiday honoring Confederate generals Robert E. Lee and Thomas J. "Stonewall" Jackson.

(The holidays were eventually separated—some might say "segregated.") Fortunately, this petty racism is becoming more of a ridiculous annoyance, or at worst a crude insult, rather than what it once was: a sign of racism that at any moment might have turned deadly.

When President Lyndon Johnson signed the Civil Rights Act of 1964 into law, he's said to have remarked to an aide, "We've just cost the Democratic Party the South for a generation." That would turn out to be an understatement. In the next election, Richard Nixon would use what he called his "Southern strategy" to make white Southerners who had voted for Democrats all their lives switch to the party that hadn't supported the civil rights movement. That strategy continues to be used, ironically by the party of Lincoln, right up to the present day, *two* generations later.

On this day in the Rose Garden, President Reagan isn't supportive of demands for civil rights, in part because he believes that you get what you earn, what you work for, and that nothing can stand in your way if you work hard enough. What he fails to understand as he smiles for the cameras, disguising his true feelings, is that King had done just that: He got what he earned.

King's extraordinary achievements, accomplished by the brilliant application of tactics and the sheer force of moral will—without once attaining power as an elected official—stand among the greatest achievements in American history. Credit also goes to the many people who preceded him, stood with him, and continued his work—much more credit than many of them receive—yet no one can say King receives more than his due. His vision of the benefits to *all* Americans of a country with true equality is now so widely understood and shared that it has become a common dream—and more real than ever. ┄

King in 1964 at a press conference at the U.S. Capitol

NOTES AND SELECTED BIBLIOGRAPHY

WORKS BY OR INCLUDING THE WRITING OF MARTIN LUTHER KING JR.:

Carson, Clayborne, ed. *The Autobiography of Martin Luther King, Jr.* New York: Warner Books. 1998.

Carson, Clayborne, et al., eds. *The Papers of Martin Luther King, Jr.: Volumes I–V*. Berkeley, CA: University of California Press, 1992–2005.

King, Martin Luther (Jr.). *Why We Can't Wait*. New York: Harper & Row, 1964.

HISTORICAL AND BIOGRAPHICAL WORKS:

Branch, Taylor. *At Canaan's Edge*. New York: Simon & Schuster, Inc., 2006.

Branch, Taylor. *Parting the Waters*. New York: Simon & Schuster, Inc., 1988.

Burns, Stewart. *To the Mountaintop*. New York: HarperCollins Publishers, 2004.

Colaiaco, James A. *Martin Luther King, Jr.: Apostle of Militant*

Nonviolence. New York: St. Martin's Press, 1988.

Davis, Townsend. *Weary Feet, Rested Souls*. New York: W. W. Norton & Company, 1998.

Deats, Richard. *Martin Luther King, Jr.: Spirit-Led Prophet*. New York: New City Press, 1999.

Frady, Marshall. *Martin Luther King, Jr.: A Life*. New York: Lipper/Penguin, 2002.

Garrow, David J. *Martin Luther King, Jr. and the Southern Christian Leadership Conference*. New York: William Morrow & Company, 1986.

Halberstam, David. *The Children*. New York: Fawcett/Random House, 1998.

Norrell, Robert J. *The House I Live In*. New York: Oxford University Press, 2005.

Oates, Stephen B. *Let the Trumpet Sound*. New York: Harper & Row, 1982.

Thernstrom, Stephen and Abigail. *America in Black and White: One Nation, Indivisible*. New York: Simon & Schuster, Inc., 1997.

NOTES

page 2, "felt keenly": Garrow, 588.

pages 5–17, bus incident: *Autobiography*, 9–11.

page 12, "We cannot have": *Autobiography*, 9. See also "The Negro and the Constitution," *Papers*, vol I. online at:

http://www.stanford.edu/group/King/publications/
papers/vol1/440500-The_Negro_and_the
_Constitution.htm

page 13, "Boy . . . show me your license": Oates, 12.

page 15, "I don't care how long": *Autobiography*, 8.

page 16, "The finest Negro": "The Negro and the
Constitution, *Papers*, vol I.

page 24, "Here the first Confederate flag": *Autobiography*, 42.

page 28, "Look, woman": Garrow, 12.

page 33, "I believe you are Reverend King": *Autobiography*,
97.

page 39, "Give us the ballot": *Autobiography*, 108.

page 43, "Fill up the jails": *Papers*, vol. V, 369.

page 44, "Fellas": Branch, *Parting the Waters*, 296.

page 46, "The defendant will rise": Branch, *Parting the Waters*,
308.

page 57, "Leadership must do this": Branch, *Parting the Waters*,
455.

page 58, "If they don't get here": Arsenault, Raymond.
Freedom Riders: 1961 and the Struggle for Racial Justice. New
York: Oxford University Press, 2006; 234.

page 66, "a monument to white supremacy": Colaiaco, 45.

page 67, "the most segregated city": Oates, 210.

page 68, "unwise and untimely": Oates, 222.

page 71, "Law and order exist" and other quotations from
"Letter from Birmingham Jail": King Jr., Martin Luther, *Why
We Can't Wait*. New York: Signet Classics, 2001, 64–84.

page 82, "the revolution": Garrow , 282.

page 83, "Five score": *Autobiography*, 223–7.

page 86, "Tell 'em about the dream": Branch, *Parting the Waters*, 882.

page 91, "In view of your low grade": Garrow, 373.

page 94, "This . . . is what is going to happen to me": Oates, 270.

page 96, "anytime, anyplace, anywhere": Colaiaco, 105.

page 99, "Now, Dr. King": Halberstam, 482.

page 102, "Name one area": from a facsimile of a literacy test, online at "Civil Rights Movement Veterans" website, accessed April 15, 2008:
http://www.crmvet.org/info/litques.htm

page 105, "When the King of Norway": Halberstam, 498.

page 106, "I want Doctor King to know": Burns, 269.

page 111, "At times history": President Lyndon B. Johnson's Special Message to the Congress: "The American Promise," March 15, 1965. From website of the Lyndon Baines Johnson Memorial Library and Museum. Accessed June 1, 2008:
http://www.lbjlib.utexas.edu/johnson/archives.hom /speeches.hom/650315.asp

page 115, "probably the strongest speech": Deats, 98.

page 125, "I believe in my heart": Garrow, 483.

page 126, "I'm sick and tired": Garrow, 485.

page 127, "I don't know what": Garrow, 488.

page 134, "I am mandated": Frady, 184.

page 137, "Nonviolence as a concept": Colaiaco, 195.

page 138, "We've got some": *Autobiography*, 365.

page 139, "a national disaster": Oates, 493–494.